How Not to be the Perfect Teenager

This is a STAR FIRE book

STAR FIRE
Crabtree Hall, Crabtree Lane
Fulham, London SW6 6TY
United Kingdom

www.star-fire.co.uk

First published 2007

07 09 11 10 08

1 3 5 7 9 10 8 6 4 2

Star Fire is part of The Foundry Creative Media Company Limited

© The Foundry 2007

The right of Ulysses Brave to be identified as the author of this
work has been asserted by him in accordance with the Copyright,
Designs and Patents Act 1988.

The CIP record for this book is available from the British Library.

ISBN: 978 1 84451 943 9

Printed in China

Thanks to: Cat Emslie, Andy Frostick, Victoria Lyle,
Sara Robson, Nick Wells

How Not to be the Perfect

Teenager

Ulysses Brave

STAR FIRE

Foreword

There are so many rules today, scrupulously compiled by faceless committees of governing and busy bodies. Over the years many people have appealed to me for clarity and purpose on such matters. They say that it is difficult to know how to behave in modern society, so I have penned some careful advice based on simple, old-fashioned common sense.

Ulysses Brave

*Skin problems can
cause great anger in the
budding teenager.*

There comes a time in every teenager's life when they simply no longer fit in their parent's car.

*Be sympathetic to the teenager's
need to build a wall of silence
around them.*

10

When your teenager sleeps late,
you will need to remind them to
look in the mirror before entering
the real world.

Singing to themselves at home is a favourite teenage occupation.

It might be difficult to persuade the teenager out of the annual bath, once they immerse themselves.

When a girlfriend you've
never seen before turns up in
your living room, try not to
be too shocked.

Teenagers are obsessed with bottoms.

If your teenager decides to rest in the middle of the day, make sure they do so in a safe place.

Older teenagers often think they know everything. Everything, that is, except good behaviour in polite company.

If your teenager lies down again, in a safe place, try not to comment on any unfortunate personal issues.

A teenage boy's greatest fear is to end up looking and behaving like their father.

How to be a Teenager
Rule No. 32:
Girls love boys
with big ears.

The best looking girls always
go around in pairs, making it
impossible to approach the
one you really fancy without
teeth-grinding embarrassment.

It is not cool to try your
Karate moves in the street,
in front of your parents.

Some teenagers really do look exactly as they feel.

Many teenagers seem to lose control of their limbs.

As a paranoid teenager, it is highly unlikely that you are being followed anywhere by anyone, at any time.

Try not to make a fool of yourself on a first date.

Teenage sex can make
you go blind. Or make
you want to.

Playing 10 hours non-stop on your game console can enhance your status as a teenager, but not your appearance.

Teenage parties are full of lonely teenagers thinking that everyone else is having a great time.

Yes, you really do look like that, but don't worry, you _will_ be a beautiful swan. No really, it always happens.

Teenage girls like to try impossibly high heels, even if it makes walking across the road, well, impossible.

Try to look beyond your teenage years. A job? A profession? OK, just keep listening to your iPod.

Wallowing in self-pity is an essential part of growing up.

To become a true teenager, yawn as often and as loudly as possible in public. Especially when being given instructions by a parent.

Actually, you <u>do</u> look gorgeous. Ready for a webcam session on your favourite internet chatroom.

Hiding in the bath is a risky
strategy because:
1. your body gets clean
2. you might be noticed by other
users of the bathroom

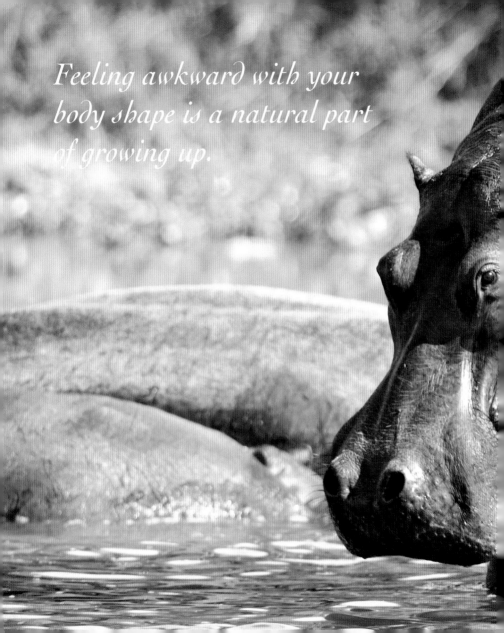

Feeling awkward with your body shape is a natural part of growing up.

Teenagers like to blend into
the background at all times.
Try not to draw attention
to them.

Toothcare is not at the top of the teenager's agenda. Stand well back after a long night's sleep.

*Don't worry if you find
some of your teenager's
friends a little scary:
they're usually just tired.*

Come back soon!